# INTRODUCTION

Kobe Bryant was more than a basketball player.

Sure, he will forever be remembered as one of the game's greatest superstars, one who burst onto the scene straight out of high school, remains fourth on the NBA's all-time scoring list, won five championships, and spent his entire 20-year career with the Los Angeles Lakers. But Kobe was also so much more.

The man known as "the Black Mamba" left his mark on the game as a fierce competitor who lifted those around him and never settled for anything less than the best. He spoke several languages, was passionate about promoting youth sports and raising his four daughters, and even won an Academy Award.

The following pages look back on Kobe's incredible life and career, from his earliest days playing the game he loved to his unforgettable 60-point final game and his desire to share basketball with everyone.

# THE LEGEND OF
# KOBE BRYANT

## Basketball's
## Modern
## Superstar

# TRIUMPH
# BOOKS

Library of Congress Cataloguing-in-Publication Data available upon request

This book is available in quantity at special discounts for your group or organization. For further information, contact:

Triumph Books LLC
814 North Franklin Street
Chicago, Illinois 60610
(312) 337-0747
www.triumphbooks.com

Printed in U.S.A.

ISBN: 978-1-62937-851-0

Content written, developed, and packaged by Adam Motin
Design and page production by Patricia Frey
Cover design by Jonathan Hahn

Photographs on pages 6, 8, 13, 14, 19, 38, 43, 50, 55, 56, 61, 62, 67, 68, 73, 74, 79, 80, 85, 86, 103, 109, and 112 courtesy of AP Images; all other images courtesy of by Getty Images
Illustrations by iStock.

"If you don't believe in yourself, no one will do it for you."

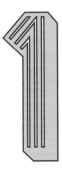

# THE LEGEND BEGINS

Kobe Bean Bryant was born on August 23, 1978, in Philadelphia. His parents, Joe and Pam Bryant, already had two daughters when they welcomed their only son into the family. Joe was an accomplished basketball player, so it wasn't a shock to anyone when Kobe started playing the game himself when he was just three years old. Naturally, his favorite team was the Lakers.

When Kobe was six, the family picked up and moved to Italy so that Joe could continue to play basketball professionally. Kobe's friend and teammate, Davide Giudici, told NBC News, "When he moved to Reggio Emilia and started playing on my team, it was immediately clear he was from another planet, a cut above us all. When he often told us that one day he would become a professional NBA player, we would make fun of him. But he worked hard for it even back then. At the end of our training, the rest of us would just go watch TV or do other things. Kobe, instead, would go home and keep training with the basket his father put up for him in his garden."

# WHAT'S IN A NAME?

Kobe Bean Bryant—not exactly an ordinary name, is it? Then again, there wasn't anything ordinary about the man who is in fourth place on the NBA's all-time career scoring list. Kobe's parents, Joe and Pam Bryant, also had two girls, Sharia and Shaya. So, how did they settle on naming their only son Kobe Bean?

According to NBA.com, the Bryants chose Kobe after seeing Kobe beef listed on a restaurant menu prior to his birth. His middle name is derived from his father's nickname, Jellybean. In high school, Joe's teammates marveled at his sweet and various moves; he recalls hearing, "It must be jelly because jam don't shake like that," a quote from a Glenn Miller song. Joe was indeed a great player and was selected in the first round of the NBA draft in 1975. Seems he may have passed down more than a name to his son!

"I create my own path. It was straight and narrow. I looked at it this way: you were either in my way, or out of it."

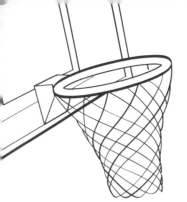

# JELLYBEAN

Kobe would grow up to become one of the greatest basketball players of all time. But his father, Joe "Jellybean" Bryant, was a very talented player in his own right.

Joe was a star forward at La Salle University and was drafted No. 14 overall by the Golden State Warriors, then traded to his hometown Philadelphia 76ers. He also played for the Clippers and Rockets during his NBA career before moving to Rieti, a small town in Italy. He later joined the team in Reggio Calabria, then in Pistoia, and ended his career in Reggio Emilia, where he was a two-time Player of the Year.

After his playing career was over, Joe coached in Europe, Asia, and the United States, including as the head coach of the WNBA's Los Angeles Sparks. But his greatest contribution to basketball is likely still raising his son, Kobe.

# PARLI ITALIANO, KOBE?

After eight seasons in the NBA, Joe Bryant moved his family to Italy to continue his playing career. Kobe was six at the time, and the Bryants lived there for many years before returning to Philadelphia when Kobe was 13.

During his years in Europe, Kobe learned to speak fluent Italian. "Italy will always be close to my heart," he said. Speaking of the town Reggio Emilia, Kobe told *BaskeTime* magazine, "I grew up here. I used to ride my bike here. There were all my friends, I have many memories, it's special."

Years later, Kobe would also learn to speak Spanish well enough to conduct interviews in that language. Was there anything Kobe couldn't do if he set his mind to it?

"You are responsible for how people remember you...or don't. So don't take it lightly. If you do it right, your game will live on in others."

# A HIGH SCHOOL PHENOM

After the Bryant family returned to Philadelphia, Kobe began a historic career at Lower Merion High School in the suburb of Ardmore. He became the first freshman in decades to start for the varsity team, though they struggled to a 4–20 record. But Kobe was never one to tolerate losing, even at that age. Over the next three years, the team went 77–13.

As a junior, Kobe averaged 31.1 points per game and was named the Pennsylvania Player of the Year. As a senior, Kobe led the team to its first state championship in 53 years and was named Naismith High School Player of the Year, Gatorade Men's National Basketball Player of the Year, and a McDonald's All-American.

Kobe had good grades and was interested in several colleges, including Duke, North Carolina, and Villanova. But in the end, he decided to forgo school and enter the NBA draft. He was ready to begin his professional career.

# THE LOGO LOVED KOBE

Few people in basketball command more respect than Lakers legend Jerry West. Need proof? The NBA's well-known logo was actually based on West's silhouette. So when the former NBA champion has a strong opinion, people tend to listen.

In 1996, West was the Lakers general manager when the team brought in a young Kobe Bryant for a private workout. After watching Kobe scrimmage for just 30 minutes, West was sold. He decided the team needed to do whatever it took to select Kobe in the upcoming NBA draft.

Michael Cooper, a former Defensive Player of the Year who guarded Kobe during that workout, told Bleacher Report, "There was no fear in him. I think that was what they were looking for."

According to former Lakers executive John Black, West said, "OK, I've seen enough. Best workout I've ever seen. He's better than anybody we have on the team right now. Let's go." It proved to be one of the best decisions West ever made.

"I see the beauty in getting up in the morning and being in pain because I know all the hard work that it took to get to this point."

# KOBE BRYANT, CHARLOTTE HORNET?

It's hard to imagine Kobe in any jersey other than the purple and gold of his beloved Los Angeles Lakers. But did you know he could've spent his NBA career in teal?

Entering the 1996 NBA draft, the Lakers had two objectives: to trade away a high-salaried player in order to free up money to offer free agent center Shaquille O'Neal, and to figure out a way to draft Kobe. The team accomplished both goals in one fell swoop, sending center Vlade Divac to the Charlotte Hornets for the rights to their 13th overall pick, Kobe Bryant. The rest is history.

Or is it? The draft was held on June 26, but the trade wasn't finalized until July 11. During that time, Divac threatened to retire rather than report to Charlotte, and some in the Hornets' world had second-thoughts about dealing Kobe. But in the end, the trade was made. Kobe would wear the purple and gold.

# DUNKS VERY MUCH

Life in the NBA is an adjustment for all rookies, especially ones used to being the center of attention. In his first season with the Lakers, Kobe was not a starter and averaged just 15 minutes per game. But if his opportunities to impress were somewhat limited, Kobe did get the chance to spread his wings at the NBA All-Star Game, where he participated in the Slam Dunk Contest.

Kobe quickly wowed both fans and judges alike, with chants of "Kobe! Kobe!" echoing through the crowd after his third dunk. After scoring a 37 out of 50 in the first round, the final round consisted of Kobe, Dallas' Michael Finley, and Minnesota's Chris Carr. Kobe pulled off a between-the-legs dunk on his first attempt as the fans oohed and ahhed. Minutes later, he was awarded the trophy, the first of many he'd lift in his incredible career.

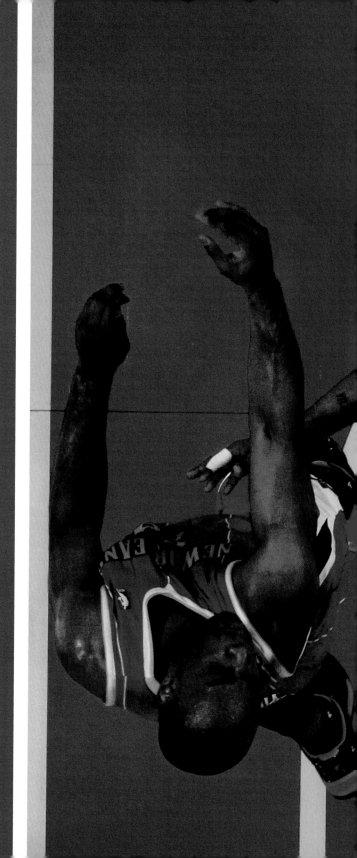

**"Losers visualize the penalties of failure. Winners visualize the rewards of success."**

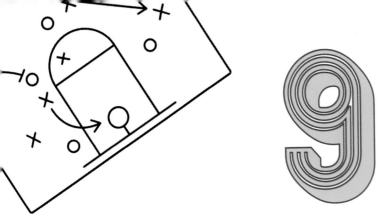

# 9

# LOVE AT FIRST SIGHT

In 1999, Kobe was a rising NBA star but was also interested in making music, something he'd done in high school. Kobe was working on his proposed solo album, while in the same building the hip-hop trio Tha Eastsidaz was filming a music video, one that featured the 17-year-old Vanessa Laine as a background dancer. In the documentary *Muse*, Kobe said, "It was a two-day video shoot, and I was always looking for her, like I wanted to know where she was. I would finish a take and go to my trailer but I would wonder where she was the entire time."

Kobe and Vanessa began dating and just six months later announced they were engaged. They got married in April 2001. Some said they were too young (Kobe was 22, Vanessa was 18), others that the NBA lifestyle would drive them apart. Neither proved to be the case, as Kobe and Vanessa were married for 18 years and had four daughters, Natalia, Gianna (Gigi), Bianka, and Capri.

# THE
# DYNAMIC DUO

Everything changed for the Lakers, and the NBA, during the summer of 1996. After a first-round playoff exit, the team acquired the rights to Kobe at the NBA draft and signed free agent center Shaquille O'Neal away from the Orlando Magic. The next basketball dynasty was born.

It wasn't always easy, though. While their playing styles seemed a perfect match on paper, off the court their relationship was complicated. Already an established star, the jovial Shaq may have seen Kobe's self-confidence as more like arrogance. Meanwhile, Kobe often complained that Shaq didn't take things seriously enough.

During their first three seasons together, ultimate success eluded them; they were swept out of the playoffs in both 1998 and 1999. It seemed like the Lakers were missing one crucial ingredient, one that would arrive the following season.

"Haters are a good problem to have. Nobody hates the good ones. They hate the great ones."

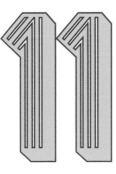

# KOBE AND THE ZEN MASTER

Phil Jackson had already coached Michael Jordan and the Bulls to six NBA championships when he agreed to become the head coach of the Lakers in 1999. Jackson was known and respected as an exceptional manager of star players and personalities, and nicknamed the Zen Master because of his philosophical approach to the game. Jackson also brought his famous triangle offense to Los Angeles, a scheme that emphasized ball movement and an equal distribution of opportunities.

Kobe and Phil had a roller coaster relationship during their years together with the Lakers. Despite his brilliant play, Kobe often complained about Jackson's "boring" offensive strategy and would infuriate the coach by refusing to follow the plays. In his book *The Last Season*, Jackson said Kobe was "uncoachable."

In the end, the two found common ground and formed a close bond. "His philosophy of the game and philosophy on life is something I've adopted, I carry it with me," Kobe said.

# TITLE NO. 1

Despite having two of the NBA's best players, the Lakers had not won a championship since the days of Magic Johnson. But with new coach Phil Jackson and a collection of veteran role players, the 1999–2000 season was shaping up to be something different.

After a hand injury sidelined him to start the year, Kobe truly came into his own, averaging 22.5 points per game as the Lakers won 67 games during the regular season. They struggled at times during the playoffs, but Kobe's clutch 25-point performance in Game 7 of the conference finals earned the Lakers a trip to the NBA Finals to meet the Pacers.

After three unsuccessful playoff seasons, the Lakers won the NBA title in six games, the first for both Kobe and Shaq. Shaq was named MVP of both the regular season and the Finals, while Kobe averaged 21 points per game in the playoffs and was named to the league's All-NBA Second Team. "We knew we had the makings to be a champion," Kobe said during the season. "We knew we had something there. In the past, we never saw that, it never happened. Teams never feared us."

At last, Kobe was a champion. But that was only the beginning.

"These young guys are playing checkers. I'm out there playing chess."

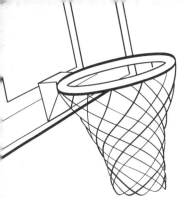

# TITLE NO. 2

If winning an NBA title is hard, it doesn't compare to winning back-to-back championships. At the time, only eight teams had won in consecutive years. Kobe and the Lakers were determined to be the ninth.

During the regular season, Kobe continued to come into his own, raising his scoring average to 28.5 points per game, but the Lakers only won 56 games, a significant dropoff from the previous season. But if other teams thought the Lakers were vulnerable, they were mistaken.

The team stormed through the playoffs, going 15–1 in the most dominant run in NBA history and winning its second championship in a row. Shaquille O'Neal was once again named the Finals MVP, but there was no doubt Kobe was a superstar in his own right, averaging 24.6 points per game and leading the team in minutes played and assists during the series.

Kobe and the Lakers had proved they were a great team. Only one question remained: could they make it a three-peat?

# 14

# THREEPEAT

Phil Jackson knew how hard it was to win three consecutive championships, having done it before with Michael Jordan and the Bulls. The Lakers would need determination, perseverance, and some heroic performances to accomplish their goal. Luckily, they had Kobe Bryant.

The Lakers rolled through the regular season, and both Kobe and Shaquille O'Neal were named All-Star starters and to the All-NBA First Team. After beating the Sacramento Kings in a controversial conference final, the Lakers beat the New Jersey Nets for their third consecutive title. Shaq was once again named Finals MVP, but it was Kobe who cemented himself as one of the game's best players in the clutch. In the fourth quarters alone, Kobe shot 63 percent from the field. At 23, he became the youngest player ever to win three championships.

But the fractured relationship between Kobe and Shaq was becoming hard to ignore. Though this wasn't their last trip to the Finals together, it would prove to be their last championship as teammates.

"I don't want to be the next Michael Jordan. I only want to be Kobe Bryant."

# KOBE AND MJ

The comparisons were hard to resist. Both Kobe and Michael Jordan were spectacular 6-foot-6 shooting guards who could dominate at both ends of the floor, make clutch shots, and were well known for their will to win. It was understandable that Kobe would pattern himself after the man many consider the Greatest of All Time. From his on-court mannerisms and fadeaway jumpers to his hatred of losing in any context, many felt Kobe was as close to being "the next Jordan" as anyone.

"When I first came into the league, Michael was terrifying everybody," Kobe said. "I was willing to challenge and learn from him. I wasn't afraid to call him and ask him questions. He was open and spoke to me a lot and helped me a lot."

In 2014, Kobe passed MJ on the league's all-time scoring list, and he retired with five NBA championships to Jordan's six. But if there's one way in which Kobe carried on MJ's legacy, it might be as an inspiration and icon to the next generation of NBA players.

# BIRTH OF THE BLACK MAMBA

Most people get their nickname from friends or family, often based on their name or personality. But Kobe wasn't most people, so he gave himself a nickname, one he'd put a lot of thought into: the Black Mamba.

In 2003–04, Kobe was struggling both on and off the court. In the documentary *Muse*, Kobe explained, "I had to separate myself. It felt like there were so many things coming at once. It was just becoming very, very confusing. I had to organize things. So I created the Black Mamba." In Kobe's mind, Kobe handled his private life, and the Black Mamba took care of business on the court.

Over the ensuing years, the "Mamba mentality" became synonymous with Kobe's passion and drive to succeed, and it was adopted as a motivating principle by teammates, opponents, and fans alike.

"I was never worried about my reputation. That's how I earned one. That's how I became the Black Mamba."

# WHAT MIGHT HAVE BEEN?

Today, it's hard to imagine Kobe wearing anything other than a Lakers jersey. But in 2004, he strongly considered switching teams and ending his Lakers career.

Kobe was a free agent and his career was at a crossroads. Phil Jackson was no longer the Lakers coach, and Kobe's relationship with Shaquille O'Neal was strained. He took a meeting with the Chicago Bulls and considered following in the footsteps of his idol, Michael Jordan. So, how close did he come to becoming a Bull? "We were looking at houses, we were looking at schools," Kobe told the *Chicago Tribune*. "We already were talking about a sign-and-trade." He also considered jumping to the Clippers, who were talking about moving from Los Angeles to Anaheim.

As it turned out, Shaq was the one who was traded, to Miami, and Kobe decided to remain a Laker.

# 8/24

Kobe was beloved in Los Angeles and one of the winningest players in franchise history, so everyone knew that one day the team would retire his jersey number. But *which* number would it be?

In high school, Kobe had worn both No. 24 and No. 33, but both of those numbers were unavailable when he joined the Lakers. So he selected No. 8, the number he wore when he played in Italy, as well as a shoutout to his number at the Adidas ABCD Camp, 143 (1+4+3=8).

In 2006, he decided to switch his number to 24, and wore it for the second half of his career.

"It's kind of a clean slate," Kobe told ESPN. "I started new. Just start completely fresh, focus on the number that meant a lot to me."

In 2017, the Lakers raised both numbers to the rafters at Staples Center, meaning no one will ever wear those numbers again. Kobe became the only player to have two numbers retired by the same team.

"We try to teach the kids what excellence looks like. We try to give them a foundation of the amount of work that it takes to be excellent."

# 81 POINTS!

Fans filing into the Staples Center on January 22, 2006, were expecting an ordinary basketball game, a contest between the Lakers and visiting Toronto Raptors. What they got instead was a historic, record-setting scoring performance from Kobe Bryant.

In leading a 122–104 comeback victory, Kobe scored 81 points, the second-highest total in league history (Wilt Chamberlain's 100-point performance in 1962 remains the highest). Kobe shot 28 of 46 from the field, scoring on a variety of jump shots, three-pointers, dunks, and free throws. Phil Jackson, who coached Michael Jordan in Chicago, said, "That was something to behold. It was another level. I've seen some remarkable games, but I've never seen one like that before."

"It really hasn't, like, set in for me," Kobe said. "It's about the 'W,' that's why I turned it on. It turned into something special. To sit here and say I grasp what happened, that would be lying."

# 20

# USA! USA!

In 1992, the United States sent the Dream Team to the Olympics, the first time NBA players had ever participated in the event. In subsequent years, the league has always tried to send its best and brightest to represent their country. It should come as no surprise that Kobe was among them.

In 2008, in Beijing, Kobe led his team to the gold medal, scoring 20 points in the final game against Spain. In 2012, in London, Kobe scored 17 points in the rematch for another American gold.

"Kobe was an outstanding and true Olympic champion," said IOC president Thomas Bach in 2020. "He embraced the power of sport to change people's lives."

In 2015, when asked about being an Olympian, Kobe said, "It carries a great honor. It goes above and beyond winning an NBA championship."

"Winning takes precedence over all.
There's no gray area.
No almosts."

# TITLE NO. 4

Just two years following the Lakers' third consecutive championship, the team imploded. Phil Jackson was fired and Shaquille O'Neal was traded. Jackson was eventually rehired, but the team he and Kobe led into 2008–09 was much different than the teams they had won with in the past.

By this point in his career, there was no doubt that Kobe was the leader of the Lakers. The team won 65 games during the regular season and reached the Finals again to face the Orlando Magic. Kobe scored 40 points in Game 1, and after the Lakers beat the Magic in Game 5 to win the title, Kobe was named the Finals MVP, the first time he'd won the award. It was also his first championship won without Shaq. Asked how important that was to him, Kobe told the *Jim Rome Podcast*, "Critical. Absolutely critical. Listen, I didn't think the criticism was fair. Magic never won without Kareem, Michael never won with Scottie. Yet, there was the criticism of, 'OK, Kobe can't win without Shaq.' Whether it was fair or not, it is what it is at that point. You've got to answer the bell. It was really, really important for me to get that done. Shaq will be the first to tell you I take great pleasure in reminding him of that."

Maurice Podoloff Trophy
2007-08 NBA Most Valuable Player Presented by KIA MOTORS
KOBE BRYANT
Los Angeles Lakers

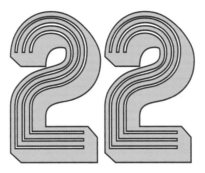

# 22

# MOST VALUABLE PLAYER

Kobe was named the MVP of the league in 2008, the only time he won that award. He averaged 26.8 points per game and led the Lakers to another championship.

So, why is it that someone as great as Kobe only won a single MVP? One reason might be that he shared the spotlight with Shaquille O'Neal for several years. Another might be that there were other great players who deserved the honor. But Kobe had his own reason, one he shared with Grantland: "Because the media votes on it. It was never a mission of mine to win a lot of MVPs. It was to win a lot of championships. With that being said, does it bother me? Yeah, it bothers me. Of course it bothers me."

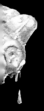

"We can always kind of be average and do what's normal. I'm not in this to do what's normal."

# TITLE NO. 5

Kobe had proven he could win a title without Shaquille O'Neal. But could he do it twice?

The NBA Finals in 2010 was a rematch between the Lakers and Celtics. The series went back and forth until Game 7. The Celtics led by 13 in the third quarter but the Lakers came back for a 83–79 victory and another championship. Kobe scored 10 of his game-high 23 points in the fourth quarter and was named the Finals MVP for the second time.

In 2015, when he was asked on TNT which of his five titles meant the most to him, Kobe said, "I think the standard answer should be, 'No. They're all the same.' But that's just not true. When we beat Boston in 2010, for me, that's number one with a bullet. Going up against three sure Hall of Famers, being down in the series 3–2, having lost to them in 2008. Understanding the history of the rivalry and all that goes on there. Having a broken finger and playing with a cast. All those things make that championship more special than the rest."

It also gave him one more championship than his old teammate, Shaquille O'Neal, who had won a fourth title with Miami.

# A FASHION ICON

Sure, Kobe always looked cool in the purple-and-gold uniform of the Los Angeles Lakers. It's one of the best and most popular ensembles in all of sports. But what did he wear off the court?

Kobe was still a teenager when he broke into the NBA in 1996, so understandably he often dressed in baggy sweats or oversized Michael Jordan jerseys. But as he got older and more comfortable in the bright lights of Los Angeles, Kobe stepped up his fashion game, choosing sleek, tailored suits more fitting of a hip businessman. Like everything else Kobe did, he took his fashion seriously. As Jim Moore of *GQ* told *The New York Times*, "He loved clothes, but he's competitive, he wants to learn from the experience."

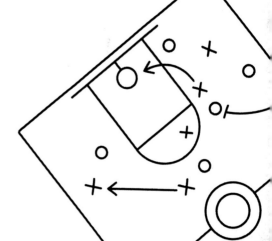

"We all have self-doubt. You don't deny it, but you also don't capitulate to it. You embrace it."

# KOBE GOT BUCKETS

Kobe could do it all on the court: pass, defend, rebound, and will his team to victory. But if there's one thing that separated him, one thing he did the best, it was score.

Kobe is in fourth place on the NBA's all-time scoring list, a position he is likely to hold for quite some time; the closest active player with a chance to catch him is Kevin Durant, who is 17,000 points behind. The only players to score more than Kobe are Kareem Abdul-Jabbar, Karl Malone, and LeBron James.

Kobe also won two scoring titles during his career, averaging 35.4 points per game in 2005 and 31.6 in 2006. In 2002, he scored more points than anyone else but had a slightly lower average, and in 2011, he lost the closest scoring race in history to Durant.

And don't forget about that 81-point night against Toronto!

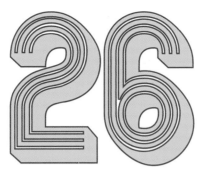

# 26

# ALL-STAR
# KOBE

Kobe always shined when the lights were brightest, and the annual All-Star Game was no exception. Kobe was named to 18 consecutive All-Star teams, the second-most all time behind Kareem Abdul-Jabbar's 19. He was also the youngest player ever to be a starter, at just 19 years old.

He was named the All-Star Game MVP four times; no one has ever won more. The 2011 game was played at Staples Center, the perfect setting for Kobe to win his fourth award. With the hometown fans behind him, he scored 37 points to lead the West over the East, 148–143.

Life is too short to get bogged
down and be discouraged.
You have to keep moving."

# BOTH ENDS OF THE COURT

When most people think about Kobe on the court, they start with his incredible ability to score, the 81-point performance against Toronto, the alley-oop to Shaquille O'Neal in the NBA Finals, and so on. But don't forget about everything Kobe did on the other end of the court.

Blessed with great size, athleticism, and determination, Kobe was a spectacular defender. He was named to the NBA All-Defensive First Team nine times, and the Second Team three times. Not bad for a guy who was often the Lakers' primary scoring option!

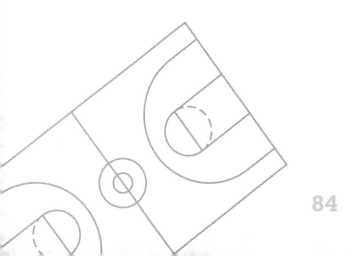

# 28

# ONE LAST TIME

The final game of Kobe's career was going to be unforgettable, no matter what the outcome was. But even Kobe himself could not have imagined a better ending.

The Lakers trailed the Jazz by 10 points with 2:36 left in the game, but Kobe refused to quit. He scored 12 straight points, including the game-winning basket with 30 seconds to go. He finished the game with 60 points, by far the most ever in a player's final game.

The crowd was going wild as his teammates celebrated around him. When it was over, Kobe said good-bye to the fans.

"This has been absolutely beautiful," he said. "I can't believe it's come to an end. You guys will always be in my heart. From the bottom of my heart, thank you. Mamba out."

# "I can't relate to lazy people. We don't speak the same language."

# IT'S ALL ABOUT
# THE SHOES

Most great players have a signature line of basketball shoes, and Kobe was no exception. Kobe signed an endorsement deal with Adidas before he was even drafted. Ten years into his career, he switched to Nike. His first release was a standard-looking basketball shoe, but over the years they evolved into a low-top sneaker more similar to something soccer players wear.

"I don't focus on how fashion changes. I only focus on creating innovative product," Kobe told ShoeCollector.com. "Hopefully the consumer knows by now that if you're buying a Kobe product, you're buying something that's been thought through. We pay attention to detail all the way through. You're buying something that's going to help you perform better."

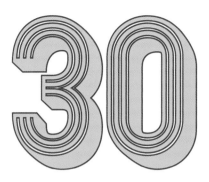

# KOBE WAS AN INSPIRATION

Kobe and Michael Jordan were similar in many ways on the court. Off the court, each inspired the next generation of players who looked up to them as role models. Most of the players in the NBA today were too young to remember MJ, but they all remember watching Kobe.

"I wanted to be just like Kobe," said Celtics forward Jayson Tatum in 2018. "He's the biggest reason I started playing basketball."

Philadelphia's Joel Embiid said on Twitter, "I started playing ball because of KOBE after watching the 2010 finals. I had never watched ball before that and that finals was the turning point of my life."

Even LeBron James said, "I grew up watching him, admiring him. I was one of the kids who came from high school. He did it. It's so surreal for me as a kid from Akron to have a guy like Kobe take time out of his day. Even at this point of my career it's still special."

"I focus on one thing and one thing only: that's trying to win as many championships as I can."

# 31

# THE GREATEST LAKER

The Lakers have been lucky to have so many great players throughout their history, from Jerry West to Magic Johnson to LeBron James. But who is the greatest Laker of all time?

Kobe has a strong case to make. He is the team's all-time leader in games, minutes, and points; won five championships; and spent his entire 20-year career in Los Angeles. When the team retired his jersey numbers in 2017, Magic made his opinion known, saying Kobe was "the greatest who's ever worn the purple and gold."

Lakers owner Jeanie Buss said, "Kobe, I thank you for staying loyal to the purple and gold, and remaining a Laker for life when it might have been easier to leave. We asked for your hustle and you gave us your heart, which was so much more."

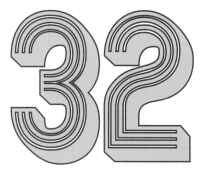

# MAMBA ACADEMY

As a father, Kobe took great interest in the teaching and training of kids and young athletes. In 2018, Kobe announced the planned opening of the MAMBA Sports Academy. A 100,000-square-foot facility in California, the Academy has basketball courts, volleyball courts, batting cages, a jiu jitsu school, and much more.

"Sports Academy has perfected the art and science of athletic training, from elite players to young kids getting started," Kobe said. "MAMBA Sports Academy is a natural expansion of my commitment to educating and empowering the next generation of kids through sports."

"Leave the game better than you found it. And when it comes time for you to leave, leave a legend."

# KOBE WINS AN OSCAR

Many questioned what someone as driven and accomplished as Kobe would do after his playing career was over. Would he become an analyst on TV? Try to buy an NBA franchise of his own? Take a long-deserved vacation to a tropical island? But in typical Mamba fashion, Kobe decided to go his own way and worked with former Disney animator Glen Keane on a short film titled *Dear Basketball*.

The animated short, based on the letter Kobe wrote in announcing the 2015–16 season would be his last, features pencil drawings by Keane, narration by Kobe, and music by *Star Wars* composer John Williams. It won the Academy Award in its category at the 2018 Oscars, proving once again there was nothing in the world Kobe could not conquer.

# KOBE AND GIGI

When the news broke that a helicopter carrying Kobe, his daughter Gigi, and seven others had crashed outside of Los Angeles, it seemed like the whole world came to a stop. Gigi had taken after her dad and fallen in love with basketball, and they were on their way to one of her games when the accident happened. Everyone began sharing their memories of Kobe, and fans gathered at Staples Center to pay their respects.

Several days later, Vanessa Bryant posted on Instagram: "I take comfort in knowing that Kobe and Gigi both knew that they were so deeply loved. We were so incredibly blessed to have them in our lives. I wish they were here with us forever. They were our beautiful blessings taken from us too soon."

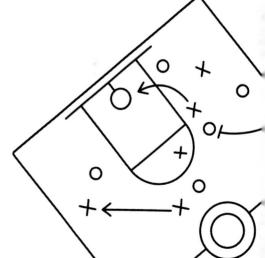

"The most important thing is to try and inspire people so that they can be great in whatever they want to do."

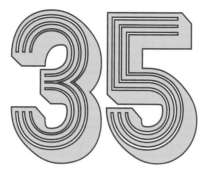

# THE HALL
# OF FAME

There was no doubt Kobe would be inducted into the Hall of Fame after his career was over. After all, he was one of the greatest basketball players of all time. The NBA and the Hall itself made it clear that nothing had changed after the helicopter accident.

HOF chairman Jerry Colangelo told The Athletic, "Expected to be the most epic class ever with Kobe, Tim Duncan, and Kevin Garnett. Kobe will be honored the way he should be."

Kobe will become the 27th member of the Hall of Fame to have played for Los Angeles. It will be a well-deserved honor for the greatest Laker of them all.

"I'm reflective only in the sense that I learn to move forward. I reflect with a purpose."